TOUGH COOKIES

A One-Act Play

by

Edward Crosby Wells

FOUNDED 1830

New York Hollywood London Toronto

SAMUELFRENCH.COM

Copyright © 2007 by Edward Crosby Wells

ALL RIGHTS RESERVED

CAUTION: Professionals and amateurs are hereby warned that TOUGH COOKIES is subject to a royalty. It is fully protected under the copyright laws of the United States of America, the British Commonwealth, including Canada, and all other countries of the Copyright Union. All rights, including professional, amateur, motion picture, recitation, lecturing, public reading, radio broadcasting, television and the rights of translation into foreign languages are strictly reserved. In its present form the play is dedicated to the reading public only.

The amateur live stage performance rights to TOUGH COOKIES are controlled exclusively by Samuel French, Inc., and royalty arrangements and licenses must be secured well in advance of presentation. PLEASE NOTE that amateur royalty fees are set upon application in accordance with your producing circumstances. When applying for a royalty quotation and license please give us the number of performances intended, dates of production, your seating capacity and admission fee. Royalties are payable one week before the opening performance of the play to Samuel French, Inc., at 45 W. 25th Street, New York, NY 10010 or to Samuel French (Canada), Ltd., 100 Lombard Street, Lower Level, Toronto, Ontario, Canada M5C 1M3.

Royalty of the required amount must be paid whether the play is presented for charity or gain and whether or not admission is charged.

Stock royalty quoted upon application to Samuel French, Inc.

For all other rights than those stipulated above, apply to Samuel French, Inc. 45 West 25th Street, New York, NY 10010.

Particular emphasis is laid on the question of amateur or professional readings, permission and terms for which must be secured in writing from Samuel French, Inc.

Copying from this book in whole or in part is strictly forbidden by law, and the right of performance is not transferable.

Whenever the play is produced the following notice must appear on all programs, printing and advertising for the play: "Produced by special arrangement with Samuel French, Inc."

Due authorship credit must be given on all programs, printing and advertising for the play.

ISBN **978-0-573-65131-1**   Printed in U.S.A.   #22303

No one shall commit or authorize any act or omission by which the copyright of, or the right to copyright, this play may be impaired.

No one shall make any changes in this play for the purpose of production.

Publication of this play does not imply availability for performance. Both amateurs and professionals considering a production are strongly advised in their own interests to apply to Samuel French, Inc., for written permission before starting rehearsals, advertising, or booking a theatre.

No part of this book may be reproduced, stored in a retrieval system, or transmitted in any form, by any means, now known or yet to be invented, including mechanical, electronic, photocopying, recording, videotaping, or otherwise, without the prior written permission of the publisher.

IMPORTANT BILLING AND CREDIT REQUIREMENTS

All producers of *TOUGH COOKIES* must give credit to the Author of the Play in all programs distributed in connection with performances of the Play, and in all instances in which the title of the Play appears for the purposes of advertising, publicizing or otherwise exploiting the Play and /or a production. The name of the Author *must* appear on a separate line on which no other name appears, immediately following the title and *must* appear in size of type not less than fifty percent of the size of the title type.

Tough Cookies was first presented on October 21, 1988 by New Mexico Repertory Company's Theatre-in-the-Making at the Rep East Theatre, Albuquerque, NM. The Set Designer was Barbara Bock, the Lighting Designer was Paul Ford, the Photographer was Ron Perkins and the Stage Manager was Alan Ware. The production was directed by Barbara Bock with the following cast:

        JO   Dolores Gravning
        BILLIE   Jean Thompson
        MAMMAW   Penny Powell

Tough Cookies was the winner of the 1991 Festival of New Plays sponsored by The Society for Theatrical Artists' Guidance & Enhancement (S.T.A.G.E.) Dallas, Texas and was produced by STAGES '91 at the Dallas Museum of Art in August 1991.

CHARACTERS

JO — A woman in her early fifties to mid-sixties.
BILLIE — Jo's friend and neighbor, the same age as Jo.
MAMMAW — (pronounced ma'am-ah) Jo's Mother.

SETTING

Jo's kitchen. It is clean and well-organized. The actual design of the set can be very simple, requiring only the following: EXITS stage left and right, a kitchen table and three chairs, a curtained-window unit downstage left or right for the actors to look out, an ironing board and a basket of clothes downstage opposite the window unit. Upstage is a cart with a coffee pot, a counter containing two standing plates, one with the face of Elvis Presley and the other with the face of Jesus. There is also a telephone and somewhere a small trash can. This all works well against a black-curtained backdrop. That's the bare bones.

(AT RISE — Elvis Presley is playing on the radio. BILLIE, a large bulk of a woman, her hair in rollers, is seated at the kitchen table, painting her toenails and sometimes knitting.

JO is slender by comparison and prone to move about the kitchen bird-like—pecking here and there, searching for something to clean, to polish, something to do. It is not JO's impulse to remain idle for very long. In her forever-scrutinizing eyes, it is her duty as a housewife to see that all the household chores are done and when they are, it is her duty to create new ones—however mundane they may be. She wears a cobbler's apron filled with all sorts of cleaning supplies that she uses, more often than not, throughout the course of the play.)

JO. *(Running her hands down along the curtains hanging on the kitchen window—sighs and nods negatively.)* I don't know. Honest to God, I really just don't know.

BILLIE. *(Stops polishing her toenails.)* What kind of material did you have in mind?

JO. Don't know that I had any kind in mind, Billie. (Crosses to turn off radio.)

BILLIE. *(Sips coffee.)* You'll be wanting something cheery.

TOUCH COOKIES

JO. Why?
BILLIE. All right... you want something gloomy and dingy and ugly as sin, right?

(Picks up her knitting.)

JO. You go to such extremes.
BILLIE. You want my input or not?
JO. Input? I don't even like the sound of that!

(Dusting something.)

BILLIE. Input is a perfectly good word. It means putting in ones—
JO. *(Cutting her off.)* Two cents?
BILLIE. *(Unruffled.)* Putting in ones ideas about a thing.
JO. You mean opinion.
BILLIE. Well, yes. You could say that.
JO. Why didn't you?
BILLIE. *(Sips coffee. After a pause.)* What's wrong with the ones you got, anyway?
JO. Whoever said there was anything wrong with them?
BILLIE. Excuse me, but I'm sure I heard somebody say not two minutes ago, in this very room, she wanted to change the curtains in that there window.
JO. That don't mean there's got to be something wrong with them. I'm just tired of looking at them, that's all.
BILLIE. *(After a pause to study curtains.)* Hmmm... oh... well... maybe you're right, Jo. I don't know.
JO. *(Polishing something.)* You don't know what?
BILLIE. I don't know if I'm tired of looking at them or

TOUCH COOKIES

not.

JO. Why should you be?

BILLIE. I see those curtains often enough, don't I?

JO. Not half as much as me.

BILLIE. No, not nearly so much.

JO. Then, who cares? I'm the one who's got to look at them day and night. Not you. You can go next door and look at your own curtains. You don't got to live with them like I do.

BILLIE. No. Not like you do. Sorry.

(Rises and goes to cabinet, looking for something.)

JO. Who cares... that's all I've got to say. Who cares? *(Watching BILLIE.)* Now what?

BILLIE. Something to nibble on with my coffee. Acid. One should never drink too much coffee all on its own—too much acid.

JO. *(Reaches into a nearby cabinet and removes a plastic container filled with sugar cookies—handing BILLIE the cookies.)* Here. I made these yesterday.

BILLIE. *(Returning to table.)* Sugar cookies! My favorite.

JO. You say that about all cookies.

BILLIE. I do not.

JO. You do too. Last week peanut butter cookies were your favorite. The week before that it was tollhouse.

BILLIE. Oh, I love tollhouse.

JO. See what I mean?

BILLIE. Well... next to tollhouse, sugar cookies are my absolute favorite.

JO. Rats', too.

BILLIE. Rats?

TOUCH COOKIES

JO. That's what I put down for the rats.

(Gets coffeepot.)

BILLIE. You feed your rats?
JO. I don't have any rats—not anymore... coffee?
BILLIE. Please. Delicious. *(Polishing off a cookie.)* You must give me your recipe.
JO. *(Pouring coffee.)* The one for people or the one for rats?
BILLIE. For people, of course. I don't have rats.
JO. You don't?
BILLIE. No. The very idea—
JO. *(Returning coffeepot to counter.)* They had to come from somewhere.
BILLIE. If you're hinting that I have rats and that they somehow carpet-bagged their way over here under my fence, you're sadly mistaken. What about Clara on the other side? They could've come from her, you know.
JO. Clean as she is? Don't be silly.

(Sits at table.)

BILLIE. Well, I don't have rats. I never did have rats. And, I certainly don't intend to get any! But, if I did, I wouldn't be feeding them cookies. Poison. I'd feed them poison. *(Pauses to examine cookie.)* Jo, what's the difference between the people recipe and the rat recipe?
JO. Margarine instead of butter.
BILLIE. Practical.
JO. Imitation vanilla extract.

TOUCH COOKIES

(Sips coffee.)

BILLIE. Smart. Why waste the real thing on rats.

JO. And an extra cup of sugar.

BILLIE. *(Nibbling on another cookie.)* They like them sweet, huh?

JO. How would I know? The extra sugar counteracts the taste of the poison.

(Rises—starts dusting.)

BILLIE. How would you know that? I mean, it could be sweet already. It seems to me, if you're going to make a poison, you're going to make it attractive to the thing you wanna kill. *(Nibbles on cookie.)* Maybe the extra sugar counteracts the taste of the cheese.

JO. What cheese?

BILLIE. In the rat poison.

JO. There ain't no cheese in the rat poison.

BILLIE. How do you know? Did you taste it?

JO. *(Through clenched teeth.)* No, I didn't taste it.

BILLIE. *(Slyly.)* Well, you ought to. *(Nibbles cookie.)* I bet it tastes like cheese.

JO. It could taste like chicken fried steak, for all I care.

BILLIE. That's it! I'll make chicken fry for dinner. Thanks, Jo.

JO. Don't mention it.

(Sits at table.)

TOUCH COOKIES

BILLIE. So, instead of sugar on the top, you sprinkle on a little rat poison.

JO. No. I mix it in with the batter—a lot of rat poison.

BILLIE. *(Spitting out cookie. The soggy crumbs fly across the table.)* What?

JO. Look at the mess you're making! *(Starts to wipe table with towel.)* You don't really think I'm going to feed my best friend cookies I baked for the rats, do you?

BILLIE. *(A moment to think.)* No.

JO. Then stop acting like a retard! Look what you went and did! You got coffee and crumbs all over my arrangement. *(Examines the arrangement of plastic flowers setting on the table.)* Something else to clean.

BILLIE. *(Starts to rise.)* I'll do it.

JO. *(Motions BILLIE to remain seated.)* You just stay put. *(Rises and crosses to drawer under counter.)* I'll take care of it.

BILLIE. Okay. *(Begins to remove the rollers from her hair. After a pause.)* Any news about H.O.?

JO. *(Searching through drawer.)* Nothing more than I told you yesterday. *(Removes metal Band-Aid container, closes drawer.)* They're going to send him home tomorrow. That's all I know. *(Crosses to table, sits and removes Q-tips from container—begins to clean plastic floral arrangement with meticulous care.)* Ugh... what a filthy mess.

BILLIE. That's not all me.

JO. Billie, did I say it was?

BILLIE. No.

JO. Then don't go putting words in my mouth.

BILLIE. Did they find out what made H.O. take such a fit?

TOUCH COOKIES

JO. *(Uncomfortable with the subject.)* Some kind of stomach thing, that's all I know.

(Rises to get broom and dust pan.)

BILLIE. Well, something ain't right. I mean, a man just don't start foaming at the mouth in the middle of Tootie's and take to ripping all the plastic off all the chickens in the meat case.

JO. He said he wanted to set them free.

(Begins sweeping crumbs around table.)

BILLIE. Free? Free to do what?

JO. I don't know! Fly away, maybe.

BILLIE. Jo, frozen chickens can't fly away.

JO. *(More to herself.)* I suppose he'll be moping around the house all week expecting me to wait on him hand and foot.

BILLIE. They hop.

(Rises.)

JO. What?

BILLIE. *(Demonstrates.)* Hop, hop! Chickens kinda run and hop. I'm sure they don't fly.

JO. What on earth are you talking about?

BILLIE. Chickens. You said ol' H.O. took the plastic off so they could fly away.

JO. No, I didn't say any such thing.

BILLIE. *(Thinking back.)* Oh... I thought you did.

JO. Well, I didn't. 'Sides, they was quartered.

TOUCH COOKIES

BILLIE. Quartered? That pretty much puts an end to hopping, too, don't it?

(Sits and brushes hair.)

JO. What is wrong with you this morning? You take a stupid pill or something?
BILLIE. No. Took a water pill—bloat.
JO. Well, you better be careful. You're liable to end up with brain-rot!

(Returns broom and dust pan.)

BILLIE. *(Slams down hairbrush.)* I know you don't mean to hurt me, Jo, but you do sometimes. You know that, don'tcha? *(No response.)* Jo, is something bothering you this morning—I mean, more than usual?
JO. *(Returns to table and sits and cleans plastic floral arrangement with Q-tip.)* Ain't nothing bothering me.
BILLIE. *(Watching JO clean the flowers.)* Well, you're not yourself.
JO. Who am I?
BILLIE. Don't you know?
JO. I know I'm someone who's tired. Just tired.
BILLIE. I didn't sleep well last night, either. Sanford dog barked all night. When Georgie's home, dogs don't bark all night.
JO. Course they do.
BILLIE. Oh, no. Georgie gets out there and yells once and you don't hear another yap all night.
JO. Well, it ain't got nothing to do with sleep. I'm just tired.

TOUCH COOKIES

Tired of taking care of people. Tired of living. Tired of not living. Tired. Just tired. Don'tcha understand?

BILLIE. I guess.

JO. When's my turn, huh? I thought when we retired we were gonna do things... travel maybe. Visit some of H.O.'s folks up north.

BILLIE. Well, you can still do that.

JO. Sure... with mother to take care of?

BILLIE. Mammaw can take care of herself. God! She's got more energy than any two people I know.

JO. *(Disregarding the last.)* And Howie Boy... sending him all our extra money so he can eat and pay his rent.

BILLIE. He's nearly forty, Jo. He hadn't ought to be drainin' you so.

JO. He's a songwriter. It takes time to break into the business.

BILLIE. Still, he's too tied to his mama, if you ask me.

JO. *(Warning.)* Ain't no one asking you, Billie.

BILLIE. Sorry. *(Pause.)* You got all the cotton plumb wore off that Q-tip. *(JO frowns and takes out a fresh Q-tip. After a pause.)* What do you suppose the "Q" stands for?

JO. What?

BILLIE. The "Q" in Q-tip. What do you suppose it stands for?

JO. It don't stand for nothin'.

BILLIE. It's gotta stand for something.

JO. Why? Because you say so?

BILLIE. Quick. Quick-tip, that's it!

JO. I got things to do, Billie. I can't sit around all day like some people I know.

BILLIE. What is that supposed to mean?

TOUCH COOKIES

JO. What is what supposed to mean?

BILLIE. You think I sit around all day and do nothing, don'tcha?

JO. Why does the world always have to revolve around you, huh? You always think I'm talking about you. There are other people walking around this planet, too.

BILLIE. Then, who? Who, Jo? Who? Who did you have in mind?

JO. I don't know who! Honest to God—Miz Astor! That's who!

(Rises - throws down Q-tip.)

BILLIE. You meant me. You had me in mind.

JO. *(Squirts back of chair with cleaner taken from out her cobbler's apron, then proceeds to wipe chair dry.)* I didn't have nobody in mind, Billie. Nobody. H.O.'s coming home tomorrow and there's things to get done. You know how men are. Get a little tummy ache and it's "get me this!" and "get me that!" There ain't nothing more helpless than a grown man outta sorts.

BILLIE. Still, it's nice to have a man around the house.

JO. Why don't you just die and stay stupid!

BILLIE. Abuse me all you like, Jo. What goes 'round comes 'round.

JO. So you say.

BILLIE. It's a fact, Jo. As ye sow so shall ye reap.

JO. Don't you quote to me, missy. You wanna do that kind of thing you go down the street corner and quote to somebody who cares. Not to me... not in my house!

BILLIE. *(Demurely.)* Elvis would have agreed.

TOUCH COOKIES

JO. *(Controlled outrage.)* How dare you? How dare you?
BILLIE. Well... he would have.
JO. Don't you ever disgrace the name of Elvis Presley while you're sitting under my roof again. Elvis was a saint.

(Crosses to 'Elvis' plate.)

BILLIE. For God's sake, Jo, he weren't nothin' but a singer.
JO. A singer? A singer? *(Holding 'Elvis' plate - with maniacal restraint.)* An instrument of God, Billie. A saint among men, martyred. Taken to the Lord's breast in his prime... murdered!
BILLIE. Nobody murdered him, Jo. He did it to himself.
JO. How dare you?
BILLIE. Drugs, Jo. He took drugs.
JO. He was murdered—cut down by the American Medical Association... a branch of the Mafia!
BILLIE. *(Resigned.)* All right. Whatever you say.
JO. No. No, it's not all right because I say it. It's all right because it's the truth—and I know it.

(Dusts 'Elvis' plate.)

BILLIE. Okay, okay.
JO. Don't you ever disgrace the good name of Elvis Presley in this house ever again.
BILLIE. All right. I'm sorry, okay?
JO. Never again.

(Replaces the 'Elvis' plate and gives the 'Jesus' plate a quick flick of the duster, almost as an afterthought.)

TOUCH COOKIES

BILLIE. *(Anxious to change the subject.)* I found a penny head's up this morning. That's good luck, isn't it?

JO. *(Returning to table - sits.)* It ain't nothin' but superstitious junk! How a grown woman can believe in that kind of thing is beyond me.

(Sips coffee.)

BILLIE. I never said I believed in it. *(Gathers up her knitting and hair rollers.)* I think I'll be heading home.

JO. Why? Got something better to do?

BILLIE. Maybe.

JO. I'm sure it ain't housework.

BILLIE. *(Dropping her belongings back onto the table.)* Jo, my house is my business. You can clean and scrub and make a fool of yourself all you like. I don't care. Who've I got to clean for, huh? Georgie ain't home but three or four days a month.

JO. Well, that's what you get for marrying a rodeo man.

BILLIE. Humph.

JO. But, since you bring it up, you can't exactly eat off your kitchen floor, can you?

BILLIE. I don't know. Do you need an answer right away?

JO. You can eat off mine.

BILLIE. No, Jo. You can eat off yours. I'll stay at the table if you don't mind.

JO. It's just a figure of speech.

BILLIE. *(Stands.)* Of course it is. It's your quaint way of telling me I'm dirty.

JO. I never said any such thing.

TOUCH COOKIES

BILLIE. Not directly, no. You don't know how to be that honest.

JO. *(Stands.)* Honest? You want honest? Your house is a pig sty.

BILLIE. That's not honest. That's rude.

(Sits.)

JO. You asked for it.

(Sits and starts on flowers with Q-tip.)

BILLIE. This compulsive addiction you have for housewifery is a sickness, don'tcha know.

JO. So is living in filth.

BILLIE. Look at yourself.—polishing that there bunch of plastic flowers with a Q-tip. That's sane?

JO. It's my job.

BILLIE. Only because you make it so. Why don'tcha just dump it in the sink and run water over it?

JO. Because that's not the way to do it.

BILLIE. That's the way I'd do it.

JO. Well, that's your problem, isn't it?

BILLIE. *(Suddenly.)* Cushion!

JO. What?

BILLIE. Cushion-tip! That's what the "Q" stands for, cushion-tip.

JO. Cushion don't start with a "Q", it starts with a "C", stupid.

BILLIE. Oh, that's right. I wonder what I could've been thinking of?

TOUCH COOKIES

JO. There's no telling.

BILLIE. You're turning into an old lady, you know that?

JO. I'm fixing to say something spiteful. 'Sides, I am an old lady.

(Stands and crosses to ironing board — begins ironing a pair of H.O.'s boxer shorts.)

BILLIE. By choice. You don't need to be. *(Bites into cookie, sips coffee.)* You were the sweetest thing in grade school.

JO. Weren't we all!

BILLIE. *(Resumes knitting.)* No, Jo, you were different. Everybody liked you then. And in high school you were a regular hell-raiser and, still, everybody liked you. All those boys chasing after you. You. Not me. You—always you. I didn't even have a date for the prom.

JO. Yes, you did. H.O. took you, as I recall.

BILLIE. I took him.

JO. Same difference.

BILLIE. No, it's not. Do you know how humiliating that was? I had to buy my own corsage.

JO. He was broke.

BILLIE. He was saving up to marry you come the end of June.

JO. You knew we was engaged. And if I hadn't broke my leg falling off the running board of that stupid Packard of yours, you wouldn't even have had H.O. to go to the prom with.

BILLIE. Well, who asked you to go and try to jump on it just as I was pulling out of the driveway?

JO. You always put on the brakes before.

BILLIE. Maybe I was in a hurry that time.

TOUCH COOKIES

JO. Ain't never been in a hurry before.

BILLIE. Look, we've been over this before and we already decided it was your fault.

JO. I'm not saying it wasn't and I'm not saying it was.

BILLIE. Well, it was.

JO. I'm just saying be thankful you had somebody to go to the prom with—considering. You know, Billie, you ought to count your blessings.

BILLIE. Easy for you to say.

JO. If you had the good sense to push yourself away from the table a bit more often, maybe some of the boys might've taken a keener interest, if you know what I mean.

BILLIE. Oh, I know what you mean all right. Maybe I just didn't want to end up an old lady, waxing and polishing and Q-tipping my life away.

JO. You married George Patterson, didn't you?

BILLIE. He's different. We're more friends than anything else.

JO. Friends?

BILLIE. *(Defensively.)* That's right—friends.

JO. Billie, a husband ain't supposed to be your friend. He's supposed to be someone you cook for and clean for. Wash for and iron for. Mend for. Call the boss up and lie for. Raise children for. Get your hair done for. If you want friends, you join the Mormons.

BILLIE. Georgie never expects anything from me but me.

JO. And that's how you picked up your filthy habits.

BILLIE. He doesn't want a house-slave, if that's what you mean.

JO. Is that what you think I am?

BILLIE. Well, I wasn't referring to the First Lady.

TOUCH COOKIES

JO. Humph. You're dumber than the day you were born.

BILLIE. Then, so are you!

JO. *(After a pause to glare, she turns toward the window.)* Yellow.

BILLIE. What?

JO. Yellow! Yellow! Something wrong with your hearing? I think I want something in yellow.

BILLIE. What? A dress?

JO. No, stupid! Curtains. We was talking about curtains, weren't we?

BILLIE. Oh... well... yellow's nice. *(The PHONE RINGS.)* Telephone.

JO. I got ears, don't I? *(Crosses to phone.)* I wonder who could be botherin' me now?

BILLIE. Maybe it's H.O. calling from the hospital.

JO. *(Into phone.)* Yeah? Yeah. Yeah. No. No. No. C. C. B. No. Wouldn't you like to know. Suppose I don't want to have a nice day? Goodbye to you, too.

(Hangs up phone.)

BILLIE. Who was that?
JO. Computer.
BILLIE. Didn't think it was H.O. What did it want?
JO. Information.
BILLIE. What kind of information?
JO. The nosey kind!

(MAMMAW enters. Maybe in spite of her age - maybe because of it - it is her spunky youthfulness that strikes us first.)

TOUCH COOKIES

MAMMAW. *(Entering.)* Was that for me?

JO. Was what for you?

MAMMAW. The phone.

JO. No, mother, it wasn't for you.

MAMMAW. *(To BILLIE.)* She wouldn't tell me if it was.

JO. You know that's a lie, mother.

BILLIE. Good morning, Mammaw.

MAMMAW. *(To JO.)* You never tell me when Howie Boy calls. *(To BILLIE.)* Mornin'. Stuffin' your face again, I see.

JO. I do too. Only sometimes he don't ask for you. Sometimes he only wants to speak to his mother.

MAMMAW. Funny thing when a boy don't want to talk to his Mammaw.

JO. Well, sometimes he's in a rush.

MAMMAW. *(To BILLIE.)* That's her story. Gained some weight since I seen you last.

JO. It ain't a story, mother.

BILLIE. That was only yesterday. I took a water pill. I lost some since yesterday.

MAMMAW. That's your story. *(To JO.)* Then, who called?

JO. For your information it was a computer that called.

MAMMAW. Did it ask for you?

JO. No, mother. It didn't ask for nobody.

MAMMAW. Then how do you know it wasn't for me? *(To BILLIE.)* She does this all the time.

JO. No, I don't, mother.

MAMMAW. *(To BILLIE.)* She hordes all the mail what comes for "occupant". *(To JO, while going through discarded mail in waste basket.)* Now don't lie about that, sister.

JO. I don't know what you're talking about.

MAMMAW. That's never stopped you before. *(To BIL-*

TOUCH COOKIES

LIE.) She's got something to say about everything. Don't know a dang thing—never did. Knows more than Walter Cronkite, she does. *(Pours herself some coffee. After a pause.)* Pit bulls are eating people up left and right, don'tcha know.
BILLIE & JO. What?
MAMMAW. Munchin' people up to beat the band.
JO. Mother, they ain't doing any such thing.
MAMMAW. Don't tell me! I got eyes, don't I? *(To BILLIE.)* She thinks I'm senile. She'll be senile long before me, I'll tell you that.

(Pulls her 'special' chair to the table and sits.)

JO. You never saw a pit bull eat nothing or nobody. You don't even know what a pit bull looks like.
MAMMAW. *(To BILLIE.)* See how she talks to me? Showed the kid being eaten right there on TV in front of God and everybody.
BILLIE. Really? Why didn't somebody do something about it then?
MAMMAW. They was busy takin' pictures. That's show biz, don'tcha know.
JO. No, mother. They never showed anything like that on TV.
MAMMAW. How do you know? Were you there? They show people gettin' eaten up by all kinds o' things all the time on TV. *(To BILLIE.)* It was on the news last night.
JO. I saw the news last night and there wasn't anything about pit bulls eating people.
MAMMAW. You got up.
JO. No I didn't.

TOUCH COOKIES

MAMMAW. *(Sips coffee. To BILLIE.)* She got up.

JO. I didn't get up.

MAMMAW. You got up and went to relieve yourself.

JO. I did not relieve myself during the news, mother.

MAMMAW. Oh, you relieved yourself all right—just when they was about to show them pit bulls eating that little kid. Now, don't tell me different 'cause I know better.

BILLIE. Seems to me I heard something about that.

JO. Now don't you start!

BILLIE. Up in Roswell, wasn't it?

MAMMAW. That's right. And then there was that ball player what got himself hit by lightning and it never did come back out.

JO. Mother, you don't know what you're talking about.

MAMMAW. I do too!

JO. I saw it too, mother, and they took him off the field where he was playing that there new kind of game they got—soccer, they call it.

MAMMAW. Baseball.

JO. No, mother, they don't kick a baseball.

MAMMAW. That's right. They use a bat. And they got him under lock and key just in case that lightning decides to come out and strike a nurse or something. He's in the hospital up in Albuquerque. *(Rises and searches about the kitchen.)* I'll tell you, the moral fiber of America is worn thin and that's the truth.

JO. What are you prowling around for?

MAMMAW. *(Finds loaf of bread.)* Something to eat. *(To BILLIE.)* She never feeds me.

JO. Oh, for pity's sake.

BILLIE. Would you like a cookie, Mammaw?

TOUCH COOKIES

MAMMAW. I don't eat rat food.

(Sits - peels the crust from a slice of bread.)

JO. It ain't rat food, mother.
MAMMAW. It's why H.O.'s in the hospital, ain't it?
JO. *(Through clenched teeth.)* No, it isn't, mother.
MAMMAW. *(To BILLIE.)* I wouldn't eat those cookies if I was you.
BILLIE. *(Rises.)* Excuse me.
JO. Where are you going?
BILLIE. To the bathroom.
JO. There ain't nothing wrong with those cookies, Billie!
BILLIE. It's the water pill.

(She EXITS.)

JO. Now see what you've done.
MAMMAW. I don't know what you're talking about, sister.

(From offstage we hear the SOUNDS of BILLIE throwing up.)

JO. You made her sick.
MAMMAW. *(Rises - crossing to window.)* Well, you make me sick.
JO. Sometimes I could strangle you with my bare hands!
MAMMAW. You could chew on a Brillo pad for all I care. *(Examining curtains.)* Thought you was going to change out these curtains today?
JO. Yes, mother. Billie and I are going to the fabric store

TOUCH COOKIES

soon as I get 'round.

MAMMAW. Can I come?

JO. If you want.

MAMMAW. No. Maybe I'll just stay to home... in my room... all alone.

JO. Do what you want, mother.

MAMMAW. You'd like that, wouldn't you? Leave me alone so I can fall and break my bones while you're out galivantin'.

JO. Then come with us for God's sake!

MAMMAW. The way you drive? Be safer on roller skates. *(Looking out window.)* Utt! That ol' Tom's in the backyard again. Shoo, shoo! Remember the McGreevy boy?

JO. Tommy Lee?

MAMMAW. That's the one. He died of cat fever.

JO. He had the croup.

MAMMAW. From sleepin' with cats.

JO. You don't get the croup from sleeping with cats.

MAMMAW. Are you a doctor now?

JO. He had weak lungs, mother. He was born with weak lungs and that's what killed him. Weak lungs.

MAMMAW. Sleepin' with cats didn't help. *(Out window.)* Shoo, shoo! Go home! Scat! Utt! There's that nigger boy. Shoo, shoo! *(Yelling out window.)* Don't you go climbin' over that fence! I'll get the police on you. See if I don't! *(Turning back to JO who is crossing to window.)* Call the police, sister.

JO. *(Looking out window.)* Oh, mother, he's just getting his ball.

MAMMAW. He ought to keep his balls on his side of the alley!

JO. There. He got it.

TOUCH COOKIES

MAMMAW. What's that hangin' outta his pocket?
JO. I don't know, mother. Looks like a stick.
MAMMAW. Bet it's a jackknife!
JO. It's not a jackknife, mother.
MAMMAW. Looks like a jackknife to me. Liable to cut your throat in the dead of night.
JO. For God's sake, mother! Nobody's gonna cut anybody's throat. There. He's gone now.

(Crosses to ironing board.)

MAMMAW. He'll be back. And the next time he'll bring the whole gang with him.
JO. What gang?
MAMMAW. They run in packs don'tcha know. Robbin' and killin' and rapin'. Wanna get raped?
JO. No, mother, I don't want to get raped.
MAMMAW. Then, call the police before he gets back here with his gang.
JO. Where on earth do you get this stuff?
MAMMAW. It's the truth. Utt! There's that ol' Tom again doin' his duty. Better be careful when you go to hangin' out the wash, sister. Pile of cat shit big enough to bury your shoes in.
BILLIE. *(Entering.)* Do you have any Lysol?
JO. Now what did you do?
BILLIE. A little accident.
MAMMAW. Rat food.
JO. Honest to God! If it ain't one thing it's another!

(EXITS.)

TOUCH COOKIES

MAMMAW. *(After a pause.)* Is she gone?

BILLIE. *(Sits a table.)* Yes.

MAMMAW. *(Crossing to BILLIE. Urgently.)* They beat me.

BILLIE. No.

MAMMAW. *(Showing BILLIE the bruises on her arms.)* See these? They didn't get there by themselves.

BILLIE. I can't believe—

MAMMAW. Believe it! It's true! Call the police!

BILLIE. What?

MAMMAW. Does that stomach of yours effect your hearing?

BILLIE. No. Of course not.

MAMMAW. Then, call the police.

BILLIE. I can't do that.

MAMMAW. Fingers gone bad? Arthritis, huh?

BILLIE. No.

MAMMAW. Oh, don't talk to me about arthritis. Look at these. *(Showing BILLIE her fingers.)* Sometimes they like to get knotted somethin' awful. I'll never play the harp, I'll tell you that! Let me see yours. *(BILLIE holds out her hands.)* Fat little piggies, ain't they? Call the police.

BILLIE. Mammaw, if what you say is true, why don't you call the police?

MAMMAW. I did. They don't believe me. Some knownothin' woman cop came to investigate and ended up siding with sister. When you reach my age you don't have any rights, don'tcha know.

BILLIE. Well, what makes you think they'll believe me?

MAMMAW. You're my witness.

BILLIE. But, I never saw them beat you.

TOUCH COOKIES

MAMMAW. That don't make no nevermind. Tell them you did.

BILLIE. That would be a lie, Mammaw.

MAMMAW. Have it your way. One day when you come over here, stuffing yourself with rat food, I'll be layin' in my room all beat up and broken... dead, maybe. How are you gonna feel then?

BILLIE. I'd feel— Is this the truth?

MAMMAW. You want it on the Bible?

BILLIE. No. Of course not.

MAMMAW. Don't believe in the Good Book, huh?

BILLIE. Look, I'll have a word with Jo about it.

MAMMAW. What good do you think that'll do?

BILLIE. I'll ask her if she's ever done what you said.

MAMMAW. Sure. Go ahead and sign my death warrant!

BILLIE. I won't ask her directly, of course.

MAMMAW. I'm telling you they beat me! They kick me! They punch me! The slap me! They— *(JO enters with Lysol and bucket.)* Have a nice day.

JO. What?

MAMMAW. I said, "have a nice day."

JO. *(Hands BILLIE Lysol and bucket.)* Here.

BILLIE. Sorry.

(EXITS.)

MAMMAW. She's sorry all right. If that ol' gal had to haul ass, it'd take her two trips.

JO. Now, mother, she's a child of God just like you and me.

MAMMAW. If you're a child of God, sister, I'm throwin'

TOUCH COOKIES

in with the one downstairs!
  JO. Did you ever love me, mother?
  MAMMAW. *(After a pause to think about it.)* No.
  JO. I thought not.
  MAMMAW. They drown female nigger babies in Africa.
  JO. What are you talking about?
  MAMMAW. Unwanted offspring. They drown 'em in Africa.
  JO. Well, thank God they don't do that in America.
  MAMMAW. Yeah... aren't you lucky.
  JO. Mother, what exactly are you saying?
  MAMMAW. Got time to give me a perm this week, or do I got to go to that sissy-man on Gibson?

(Goes to ironing board and refolds JO's ironing.)

  JO. You don't need a permanent. You only had one a month ago.

(Gets scissors and magazine, clips coupons.)

  MAMMAW. Grew out.
  JO. It didn't do no such thing!
  MAMMAW. It did. I always was a fast hair grower.
  JO. Oh, mother! Your hair grows like everybody else's.
  MAMMAW. No, it don't!
  JO. It most certainly does.
  MAMMAW. It grows faster when you're older. The older you get, the faster it grows.
  JO. Then how come mine don't? I'm getting old, too, mother.

TOUCH COOKIES

MAMMAW. You ain't normal, that's why. When you're normal it grows faster. Maybe yours is retarded.

JO. It ain't retarded, mother!

MAMMAW. They say when you get old enough you can hear it growin'. *(Crosses to counter, searching.)* It don't even stop when you're dead. Hair's awful funny that way.

JO. Are you looking for an excuse to be silly this morning?

MAMMAW. No. I'm looking for my teeth. Where did you hide them?

JO. I suppose they're where you left them, mother—in the bathroom.

MAMMAW. She probably threw up on them.

JO. She didn't throw up on them.

MAMMAW. People do, you know.

(Returns to ironing board.)

JO. She didn't throw up on your teeth, mother.

MAMMAW. How do you know? Were you there? That doctor in Juarez what fitted me with those teeth said not to get foreign objects on them.

JO. Your teeth are just fine. When Billie comes out you can go in there and get them.

MAMMAW. Make me sick! *(Spits on iron.)* This ol' iron ain't puttin' out steam again. *(Looking up toward ceiling.)* And that seems to be all that ol' swamp cooler's puttin' out—steam.

JO. When H.O. gets home I'll have him take another look at it.

MAMMAW. What about the iron?

JO. I'll have him look at that, too, mother.

TOUCH COOKIES

MAMMAW. That's all he ever does is look. He ain't mechanical minded, I'll tell you that. Run some vinegar through the iron. That ought to break down the corrosion. *(A beat.)* What did you poison him for?

JO. What?

MAMMAW. You heard me.

JO. It was an accident!

MAMMAW. That's your story.

JO. I did not poison H.O.!

MAMMAW. Somebody did.

JO. Now you stop that! I didn't do no such thing!

MAMMAW. He got into the rat food just like you intended.

JO. *(Genuinely hurt.)* How can you say such a thing?

MAMMAW. True, ain't it?

JO. No! It isn't true!

MAMMAW. How'd they get switched, then?

JO. Suppose you tell me. I'm not the only one who lives in this house.

MAMMAW. You're the only one in all of Hobbs who bakes cookies for the rats.

JO. To get rid of them, mother, not for them.

MAMMAW. What's the difference?

JO. There's no use trying to make sense with you.

MAMMAW. No. Not when you're retarded.

(Re-ironing and "correcting" all of JO's ironing and folding.)

JO. I'm not retarded!

MAMMAW. Doc Sears said you was.

JO. Then, Doc Sears was a quack.

TOUCH COOKIES

MAMMAW. Oh, you shouldn't speak ill of the dead, sister. Poor man, killed himself. Treated Dickie Keefer for hemorrhoids—big as grapes, they were—then he went into the closet and hung himself. Tongue swelled up like an eggplant—big and purple. Terrible thing—hemorrhoids. That's why I don't eat eggplant.

JO. You don't eat eggplant because it gives you gas, mother.

MAMMAW. There was this travellin' show with a two-headed rattle snake come through whiles I was carryin' you and it liked to scare me to death. Give me nightmares, it did.

JO. Oh, mother, you're making this up.

MAMMAW. Am not. It had two heads big as your fist.

JO. Well, what's that got to do with me?

MAMMAW. Told you. It marked you and that's why you're retarded.

JO. I am not retarded, mother.

MAMMAW. Not all the time, no. Just some of the time... like when you poisoned H.O.

JO. I didn't poison H.O.

MAMMAW. Tell it to the judge.

JO. You stop it! Stop it right now!

(Stops clipping coupons. Rises, with scissors in hand, and crosses towards MAMMAW.)

MAMMAW. Sure is lucky Tootie ain't gonna sue. All that good chicken gone to waste.

JO. *(Shaking her fist, with scissors, at MAMMAW.)* Sometimes I could... could... *(BILLIE enters.)* kill you!

MAMMAW. *(To BILLIE, with great satisfaction.)* There.

TOUCH COOKIES

See?

    BILLIE. Jo, what's going on?

    JO. Nothing!

    MAMMAW. Don't say you didn't see that, Billie Patterson. *(Slams down iron and starts to EXIT -- turning back.)* There better not be puke on my teeth.

(EXITS.)

    BILLIE. *(After a pause.)* What was that all about?

    JO. She thinks I poisoned H.O.

    BILLIE. Did you?

    JO. You can go lay down on the highway right now, Billie Patterson!

    BILLIE. I don't mean on purpose.

    JO. On purpose or otherwise, I did not poison H.O.

    BILLIE. Does this have something to do with rat poison in the cookies?

    JO. I'm going to tell you something and I don't want it to leave this house.

    BILLIE. What?

    JO. You better sit down.

    BILLIE. *(Sitting.)* What?

    JO. I think my mother switched the cookies.

    BILLIE. *(Covering her mouth, with panic.)* Oh my God! I'm going to die, aren't I?

    JO. No, stupid! Not on you, on H.O.

    BILLIE. Then, I'm all right?

    JO. Yes, Billie. You're perfectly fine. I already threw the poisoned batch out. She's trying to kill me, Billie. She wants me dead.

TOUCH COOKIES

BILLIE. But, I'm all right?

JO. Yes. You're just fine. It's me she's trying to kill, not you.

BILLIE. Jo, I can't believe that.

JO. She's been trying to kill me for over fifty years!

BILLIE. She couldn't have been trying very hard.

JO. Would you shut up and listen to me? I think she switched the cookies around knowing I like a snack every now and again. Only, she didn't count on H.O. getting into them since he's always braggin' on not having a sweet tooth.

BILLIE. Surely they would have discovered that at the hospital, wouldn't they?

JO. Not if they weren't looking for poison.

BILLIE. What are you going to do?

JO. I don't know. I can't go to the police because she's my mother. 'Sides, I'm the one who baked them in the first place. She's an evil woman, I'm telling you that.

BILLIE. I'm sure it's all just an innocent mistake.

JO. You really want to die stupid, don'tcha!

BILLIE. What proof do you have?

JO. She murdered my father. What more proof do you need?

BILLIE. Jo, Pappaw died of heat stroke.

JO. Who knitted him that sweater in the middle of July, huh?

BILLIE. That's hardly murder.

JO. Not in the eyes of the law, maybe. But, murder just the same. She knew what she was doing.

BILLIE. I think you're being a bit unfair.

JO. You think so, huh? Daddy always loved me better than her and she knew it. She knew it and that was her way of getting

TOUCH COOKIES

back at me.

BILLIE. Jo, that is the most ridiculous thing I ever heard you say.

JO. You think so, huh?

BILLIE. I've heard you say some pretty dumb things, but that takes the blue ribbon, best of show, hands down.

JO. Side with her all you like, it don't change a thing.

BILLIE. I'm not siding with anybody, Jo.

JO. As soon as H.O. gets out of that hospital, she's going in a home. I don't care if it takes every last cent we've got she's not staying here!

MAMMAW. *(Entering.)* My mouth tastes like Lysol.

JO. What are you on about, mother?

MAMMAW. Those motor vehicle people took my license away!

JO. What has that got to do with anything?

MAMMAW. I could get in the car and get out of here, that's what! Go somewhere where people don't go throwing up on other people's teeth! *(To BILLIE.)* I drove a covered wagon 'cross Texas and now they won't even let me drive across the street.

JO. It's for your own protection. You'd only get yourself killed like you almost did last time.

MAMMAW. Because you went and bought me them slippy shoes for my birthday. I told you they was no good. Slipped right off the brakes and onto the gas pedal. Who told you to buy me them anyway?

JO. Nobody, mother. I just thought I was doing something nice.

MAMMAW. Why?

JO. What do you mean, "why?"

TOUCH COOKIES

MAMMAW. You ain't never done nothin' nice in your life.

JO. How can you say such a thing?

MAMMAW. You want me dead, don't tell me. You bought me those slippy shoes on purpose.

JO. I bought you those shoes because you was complaining about how you didn't have any shoes to wear.

MAMMAW. I had plenty of shoes.

JO. That's what I told you. Only you went on and on about how nobody ever does anything for you.

MAMMAW. Well? Do they?

JO. I've given up my life for you, mother, and I've had about all I can take!

MAMMAW. *(To BILLIE, who is nervously knitting.)* They was cheap, slippy, catalog shoes. 'Sides, they never fit me right, anyhow.

JO. Can't you let me love you?

MAMMAW. Now you stop that! You stop that right now. You hear me, sister?

JO. *(Pleading.)* I just want to love you.

MAMMAW. Stop it, I said! Don't you go play-actin' for Billie's sake. She knows better.

JO. I gave up my life for you.

MAMMAW. And I gave you life. Remember that, sister.

JO. *(Holding back her tears.)* Then, why are you trying to kill me?

MAMMAW. You got it backwards, sister. *(To BILLIE.)* Don't let her kid you. She knew they was slippy shoes when she bought them.

JO. I didn't know any such thing, mother!

MAMMAW. Sister, you can stand there and lie all you like.

TOUCH COOKIES

It don't change a thing. God knows how you hate me.

(Crosses to window.)

    JO. *(Wiping her eyes.)* I don't hate you.
    MAMMAW. Oh, yes, you do. Ain't no doubt about that. *(Shouting out window.)* Get outta that apricot tree, you Mexican hoodlum! Go! Shoo, shoo! Damn wetbacks!
    JO. *(Crosses to look out window.)* That's the Martinez boy, mother.
    BILLIE. Dorella's boy?
    JO. That's the one.
    MAMMAW. Wetbacks.
    BILLIE. Oh, no. Dorella's a teacher.
    JO. No, she ain't. You're thinking of Manny's wife.

(Crosses to ironing board and refolds the laundry that MAMMAW had previously refolded.)

    BILLIE. No, I'm not. Manny's wife is a secretary over at the high school. Dorella teaches.
    MAMMAW. *(Yelling out window.)* Go back to Pango Pango!
    JO. Mother! Will you stop making a spectacle of yourself!
    MAMMAW. Thievin' hoodlum.
    JO. He ain't but six or seven years old.
    MAMMAW. They teach them young. They got three year old pickpockets roaming the streets of Juarez. Steal everything you got if you don't keep an eye on 'em. Knife you for a chew of bubble gum.
    JO. Nobody knifes anybody for bubble gum, mother.

TOUCH COOKIES

MAMMAW. No? *(To BILLIE.)* What do you say?

BILLIE. Well... I think that's a bit extreme, Mammaw. Don't you?

MAMMAW. *(Sits and rearranges the order of JO's coupons.)* If I did, I wouldn't have brought it up. Remember the Flowers girl?

JO. Peggy?

BILLIE. June.

JO. Peggy. Peggy Flowers.

BILLIE. No. It was June. I'm certain.

JO. I'm certain it was Peggy.

MAMMAW. Christie Mae. Christie Mae Flowers.

BILLIE. Ah, yes, that was her name.

JO. Well, whoever! Died of scarlet fever.

BILLIE. Measels.

JO. Scarlet fever.

MAMMAW. Bubble gum. She swallowed bubble gum.

JO. Oh, mother!

MAMMAW. She did! She swallowed bubble gum. Got herself bound. All stuck up. Died. Some say it was suicide. *(To BILLIE.)* What do you say?

BILLIE. I don't know enough to say anything, Mammaw.

MAMMAW. Of course you don't. Never thought you did.

JO. Mother, why don't you go and lay down for awhile?

MAMMAW. No! You're gonna sneak out to the fabric store while I'm not looking.

JO. No, I'm not, mother. Please... just for a little bit while I fix us some lunch.

MAMMAW. I don't want any lunch.

JO. Then, lay down anyway!

MAMMAW. I might not wake up.

TOUCH COOKIES

JO. Of course you'll wake up.
MAMMAW. You don't know that.
JO. *(Crossing towards MAMMAW.)* Go and lay down!
MAMMAW. *(Rises. Backing away.)* No! I 'm afraid.
JO. There's nothing to be afraid of.
MAMMAW. People die in their sleep. I'm not going.
JO. Nobody's gonna die in their sleep, mother.
MAMMAW. *(Crosses to ironing board.)* How do you know? Are you a fortune teller now?

(Proceeds to, once again, refold the ironing.)

JO. Oh, for God's sake— *(BILLIE rises.)* And just where do you think you're going?
BILLIE. *(Feigning an excuse to get out of the room -- away from the mounting tension.)* Well... I thought... ah... the bathroom.
JO. Sit down!
BILLIE. I... I took a water pill and I—
MAMMAW. She's not going to pee on the floor, is she?
BILLIE. I really need to—
JO. SIT DOWN! *(BILLIE sits.)* Thank you.
MAMMAW. Sister, if she's got to pee, let her pee.
JO. She doesn't have to pee.
BILLIE. I do. I really, really do, Jo.
MAMMAW. You hear? She does. She really, really does.
JO. She don't!
BILLIE. I do.
MAMMAW. She does.
JO. She don't gotta pee! She wants to get away from you! You're making her crazy!

TOUCH COOKIES

(Sits and proceeds to rearrange the order of the coupons.)

MAMMAW. *(Crossing to BILLIE.)* Am I making you crazy?

BILLIE. No, Mammaw. It's these water pills I've been taking for the bloat.

MAMMAW. See, sister? Bloated like a blimp. It's those water pills making her crazy.

JO. It's not the water pills. It's you!

MAMMAW. I ain't never in all my life made anybody have to pee. Remember Harvey Monroe? He had bladder problems, too. They had to hook a plastic bag to him.

JO. Mother! Go and lay down!

MAMMAW. No! And you can't make me. You just don't want me around when Howie Boy calls.

JO. Howie Boy ain't gonna call today.

MAMMAW. How do you know?

JO. 'Cause it's Monday. He never calls on Monday. 'Sides, he called last night.

MAMMAW. Liar.

JO. He called last night, mother.

MAMMAW. Liar. He didn't call last night.

JO. He did too. After you went to bed.

MAMMAW. You called him.

JO. No, I didn't.

MAMMAW. Yes, you did.

BILLIE. *(Trapped between them.)* I have to pee.

MAMMAW. You thought I was asleep, but I wasn't. You called him.

JO. He had a right to know that his daddy was in the hos-

TOUCH COOKIES

pital, didn't he?

MAMMAW. You waited for me to go to bed so you could have him all to yourself.

JO. That's not true.

MAMMAW. It's true all right. You don't want him to talk to his Mammaw.

JO. You're crazy. You don't know what you're saying.

MAMMAW. Because you know he loves me more than he does you.

JO. How can you say such a thing?

BILLIE. *(Rising.)* Look, I really need to—

JO. *(Stopping her.)* Sit down!

(BILLIE sits.)

MAMMAW. *(To BILLIE.)* Do you know why Howie Boy never comes around?

BILLIE. I just want to go to the bathroom, Mammaw.

JO. *(Warning.)* Mother, stop it. *(To BILLIE.)* Go to the bathroom.

(BILLIE rises to leave.)

MAMMAW. Stay put!

(Blocks BILLIE's way.)

JO. She's got to go to the bathroom.

MAMMAW. I don't care if she's got to go to the emergency room. Sit!

TOUCH COOKIES

(BILLIE sits.)

JO. Mother, I'm gonna have you put away!

MAMMAW. Put a zipper on it, sister! *(Picking up the plastic floral arrangement. To BILLIE.)* See this ugly plastic flower thing?

BILLIE. Yes.

MAMMAW. I'm gonna bust it over your dumb skull if you budge one inch! Now. Do you know why Howie Boy never comes around here anymore?

BILLIE. No, Mammaw. Why?

JO. That cinches it! You're going today!

MAMMAW. *(Putting floral arrangement down.)* He told me.

JO. Mother, stop it! Stop it right now!

(JO and MAMMAW begin a pattern of going 'round and 'round the table like two cats about to pounce.)

MAMMAW. Told me how sister runs around in front of him in her under things.

JO. That's not true!

MAMMAW. In front of a grown man in her bra and panties.

JO. That's a lie!

MAMMAW. Trapping him in her bedroom.

JO. You goddamn liar!

MAMMAW. Seducing her own son.

JO. You're crazy.

MAMMAW. Spider! Spider! What did you think you were doing, sister?

TOUCH COOKIES

JO. You crazy old bitch!

MAMMAW. Taking baths with him till he was fifteen years old.

JO. That's a lie!

MAMMAW. Sleepin' with him when H. O. was workin' nights.

JO. You're crazy.

MAMMAW. Crazy like a fox, sister!

JO. How dare you?

MAMMAW. No wonder he prefers men to women.

JO. You don't know what you're talking about!

MAMMAW. I know what I'm talking about all right.

(Sits.)

JO. You'd do anything to get between us! You was always interfering—trying to poison him against his own mother just like you tried to poison daddy against me! Well, he's my son, not yours! You wanted a son, but you had me and you couldn't stand that, could you? So, when I had a son you tried to take him away—poison him against me—make him your own.

MAMMAW. I should've drowned you.

JO. I know. You've been telling me that all my life! Why didn't you, huh? Why, mother, why?

MAMMAW. Because you're my daughter!

JO. Since when has that ever meant anything to you?

MAMMAW. You ain't nothin' but an ingrate!

JO. Me? Me? Who takes care of you, mother? Who took you in when daddy died? You sat over in that old drafty shack and didn't eat a thing for nearly a week. You'd be dead now, if it weren't for me.

TOUCH COOKIES

MAMMAW. It weren't no shack! It was good enough for you at one time, wasn't it?
BILLIE. *(Timidly.)* Can I go now?
JO. Shut up! *(Crosses behind MAMMAW who is seated at the table.)* I should have left you there to die.
MAMMAW. Why didn't you?
JO. Because you're my mother and I... I—
MAMMAW. *(Venomously.)* You what?
JO. I love you! (Grabs towel and begins to strangle MAMMAW.) I love you! I love you! I love you!
MAMMAW. *(Sinking to the floor.)* Help! Help!

(Obviously struggling to breathe.)

BILLIE. *(Pulling JO off MAMMAW.)* Jo! Stop it! You'll kill her! *(The PHONE RINGS.)* Stop it, Jo! Stop it!

(Manages to get JO off MAMMAW. BILLIE comforts MAMMAW. JO, staggers around in a rage. She grabs the coupons and rips them up. She grabs the plastic flowers and hurls them across the kitchen. She throws the folded ironing in all directions - things fly: The laundry, the ironing board, the iron, this & that, etc.)

JO. *(While in her rage.)* When's my turn, huh? When's my turn?
MAMMAW. *(To BILLIE.)* She never was any good. Now, will you call the police?

(The PHONE continues to RING.)

TOUCH COOKIES

BILLIE. Nobody's gonna call the police, Mammaw.

JO. Oh, she's had the police here before. Don't think she hasn't.

BILLIE. Are you all right, Mammaw?

(Helping her back into the chair.)

JO. Is she all right? Is she all right? What about me, huh? What about me? Jesus Christ! What about me?

BILLIE. *(Grabbing JO - trying to calm her.)* Jo, get hold of yourself. *(JO pulls away.)* Why don't you answer the phone, Jo?

JO. When I'm good and ready! I'll answer the goddamn phone when I'm good and goddamn ready! *(Picks up the phone.)* Yeah?

BILLIE. *(Comforting MAMMAW.)* You want to go to your room?

MAMMAW. No. Now do you see what I have to put up with?

BILLIE. Yes, Mammaw. Do you want something to drink... eat?

MAMMAW. Is that Howie Boy she's talkin' to?

BILLIE. I don't know, Mammaw.

JO. *(Into phone.)* When? Are you sure?

MAMMAW. I bet that's Howie Boy. *(To JO.)* If that's Howie Boy, you better let him talk to his Mammaw!

JO. *(Into phone.)* Yes, I understand.

MAMMAW. Don't you hang up that phone without me talkin' to him!

JO. *(Into phone.)* Thank you.

TOUCH COOKIES

(Hangs up phone.)

MAMMAW. *(To BILLIE.)* See? She did it again.

JO. Did what, mother?

MAMMAW. Talked to Howie Boy and pretended I didn't exist.

JO. That wasn't Howie Boy, mother. It was the hospital.

MAMMAW. Was it for me?

BILLIE. Is everything okay?

MAMMAW. I bet it was for me.

JO. It's H.O. They're operating on him right now.

MAMMAW. Now what did you do to him?

JO. I didn't do nothing, mother. That stomach thing turned out to be appendicitis.

BILLIE. Oh, dear.

JO. Will you drive me to the hospital, Billie? My nerves have had all they can stand for one day.

BILLIE. Certainly. You want to go right now?

JO. If you don't mind, yes.

MAMMAW. Since you're not driving, can I come?

JO. Yes, mother. If you want to come, come.

MAMMAW. *(Rises to EXIT.)* Just let me get my bag. *(Turning back.)* Remember Piggy Smith?

JO. No, mother. Who's Piggy Smith?

MAMMAW. Oh, just someone I knew once. He used to charge a nickel to let you see his appendix scar.

JO. Mother.

MAMMAW. All right, all right. I'll just be a minute.

(EXITS.)

TOUCH COOKIES

BILLIE. *(Gathering up her knitting and her hair rollers.)* Is H.O. going to be all right?
JO. Yes, I think so.
BILLIE. And you?
JO. I'm fine, Billie. Just fine. Let's go. *(BOTH start to EXIT - JO turns back and looks toward the window.)* Maybe next year. We'll wait till next year, Billie.
BILLIE. Next year? What are you talking about, Jo?
JO. Curtains. We were talking about curtains, weren't we?
BILLIE. Yes. We were.
JO. Well, we'll hold off on new ones. For awhile, anyway.
BILLIE. Sure, Jo. Anything you say. I'll get the car.

(EXITS.)

JO. *(Alone. She crosses to window and gently touches the curtains.)* Maybe... maybe in the spring. I mean, they're not bad. Not really. Not all bad. A little worn, perhaps. A little frayed. But, they're familiar—comfortable. Easy to come home to. Easy on the eye. I mean, they still have some wear in them. Some life. Don'tcha think?

(Slow FADE to BLACK perhaps to the music of Elvis Presley's "Don't Be Cruel.")

END OF PLAY

TOUCH COOKIES

PROPERTY PLOTS

JO
Carpenter apron with cleaning supplies
Feather duster
Spray bottle
Rubber kitchen gloves
Kitchen towel
Bucket
Bottle of Lysol
Magazine, scissors, and coupons

BILLIE
Hair rollers
Knitting bag with yarn and needles
Cosmetic bag with nail polish
Cup of coffee

TOUCH COOKIES

SET PLOT

Radio
3 coffee mugs
Plastic container with sugar cookies
Coffee maker with pot
Plastic flower arrangement
Band-Aid container with Q-Tips
Plate with a decal of Elvis on a stand.
Plate with a decal of Jesus on a stand.
Large men's boxer shorts
Laundry basket with clothes
Iron and ironing board
Folded clothes on ironing board
Telephone
Waste basket with junk mail and trash
Loaf of bread

EDWARD CROSBY WELLS (Playwright), born in upstate New York, began playwriting shortly after the life-altering experience of seeing the original Broadway production of Albee's *Tiny Alice*. "I had never heard words constructed in such a manner as to open places within me I never knew existed. It was as if hearing the voice of God." After playing at playwriting for many years he finally found his voice and hasn't stopped writing since. Wells has had scores of plays produced from coast to coast in the U.S. and in Europe. He is a three-time winner of the Spotlight On Best Play Award for Excellence in Off-Off Broadway Theatre and a member of The Dramatists Guild of America.

From the Reviews of
TOUGH COOKIES...

"Wells' dialogue is snappy, clean and often very funny. He has a talent for writing lines for his characters that rarely miss their marks. Whether it is outrageous humor or cutting cynicism, Wells is always on target. TOUGH COOKIES may be one of the best small plays performed on an Albuquerque stage . . . a beautiful script . . . great characters. The plot is quirky, intimate and black, suggesting the work of Beth Henley and Joe Orton . . . holds essential truths . . . the essential truth about human frictions rings true beneath the acid silliness. Wells shows talent for offbeat dialogue that makes heavy themes bearable."
—*ALBUQUERQUE JOURNAL*

"TOUGH COOKIES is a slice-of-life story of a woman trying to live under the senile wing of her mother. In the middle of the conflict sits Billie, attempting to make sense of the vicious maternal relationship. The script is teaming with malicious comments and accusations between mother and daughter, often to the point of a sick reality. Wells' dialogue is clever and witty."
—*NEW MEXICO DAILY LOBO*

". . . another response to Americans' seemingly bottomless love of black-hearted, foul-mouthed elderly female characters."
—*DALLAS TIMES HERALD*

". . . a family sitcom with emotions that essentially explode the form . . . it's as if Mr. Wells removed Aunt Pearl and her poisoned bitter pills from Greater Tuna and set her loose on the rest of the family. This is camp Southern-gothic taken to an extreme . . . ."
—*THE DALLAS MORNING NEWS*

"TOUGH COOKIES is a powerful hour of theater, exploring jealous love and hatred . . . an extraordinary play.
—*CORRALES COMMENT*

www.ingramcontent.com/pod-product-compliance
Lightning Source LLC
Chambersburg PA
CBHW071845290426
44109CB00017B/1925